HOW DOES A LIGHT BULB WORK?

By Demi Jackson

Gareth Stevens
PUBLISHING

Please visit our website, www.garethstevens.com. For a free color catalog of all our high-quality books, call toll free 1-800-542-2595 or fax 1-877-542-2596.

Library of Congress Cataloging-in-Publication Data

Jackson, Demi, author.
 How does a light bulb work? / Demi Jackson.
     pages cm — (Everyday mysteries)
 Includes index.
 ISBN 978-1-4824-3817-8 (pbk.)
 ISBN 978-1-4824-3818-5 (6 pack)
 ISBN 978-1-4824-3819-2 (library binding)
 1. Light bulbs—Juvenile literature. I. Title. II. Series: Everyday mysteries.
 TK4351.J33 2016
 621.32'6—dc23

                           2015021551

Published in 2016 by
Gareth Stevens Publishing
111 East 14th Street, Suite 349
New York, NY 10003

Copyright © 2016 Gareth Stevens Publishing

Designer: Katelyn E. Reynolds
Editor: Kristen Nelson

Photo credits: Cover, p. 1 Christina Richards/Shutterstock.com; pp. 3–24 (background) Natutik/Shutterstock.com; p. 5 Dmytro Vietrov/Shutterstock.com; p. 7 Steve Lovegrove/Shutterstock.com; p. 9 gosphotodesign/Shutterstock.com; p. 11 erashov/Shutterstock.com; p. 13 Chones/Shutterstock.com; p. 15 Alta Oosthuizen/Shutterstock.com; p. 17 bestv/Shutterstock.com; p. 19 Oleg Vinnichenko/Shutterstock.com; p. 21 Macrovector/Shutterstock.com.

Printed in the United States of America

CPSIA compliance information: Batch #CW16GS: For further information contact Gareth Stevens, New York, New York at 1-800-542-2595.

CONTENTS

Boldface words appear in the glossary.

Light Up!

When you walk into a room and turn on a lamp, how does the light bulb light up? It's powered by electricity. Electricity is a kind of **energy**. We can't see it, but we know it's working when the lights come on!

Electricity is created in power plants. It travels to our homes through big **wires** called power lines. The wires inside a house or building carry the electricity to outlets—and light bulbs! Electricity can also come from a **battery**.

Lamps and Loops

A light bulb fits into a **socket** on a lamp. This creates a circuit, or a path that connects two points so electricity can flow between them. Most people use round light bulbs called **incandescent** light bulbs.

The Main Parts

There are three main parts of a light bulb. The metal base fits into the socket. It **conducts** electricity. There's also the bulb and a thin wire called the filament. The bulb keeps the filament safe.

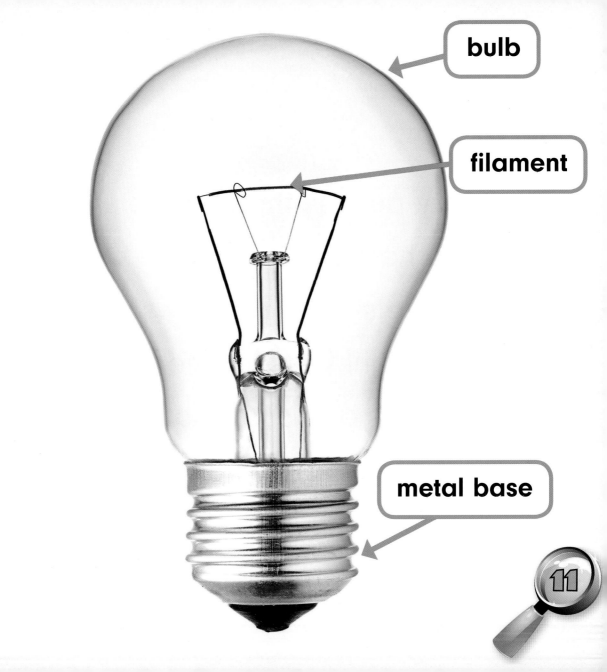

bulb

filament

metal base

11

Hot!

Electricity pushes through the filament, heating it up. The filament gets so hot it glows! This is the light we see. The inside of the bulb is a **vacuum** so the filament doesn't burn up too fast.

Have you ever touched a light bulb that's been on awhile? It's hot! Incandescent light bulbs aren't very **efficient**. Much of the electricity they use becomes heat, not light. Incandescent light bulbs also don't last very long and can break easily.

CFLs

Compact fluorescent light bulbs (CFLs) are much more efficient light bulbs! They're made up of a metal base and a glass tube filled with a gas called argon. Fluorescent lights give off light when electricity flows through the gas in the glass tube.

glass tube

metal base

17

Most of the energy powering a CFL is used to make light. Hardly any is lost in heat. That makes CFLs able to work with less energy than incandescent light bulbs. They cost more, though.

Most Efficient

A light bulb even more efficient than a CFL may be in many homes soon! LED light bulbs are already used in clocks, cell phones, and holiday lights. These light bulbs could last 20 years in a lamp!

HOW INCANDESCENT LIGHT BULBS WORK

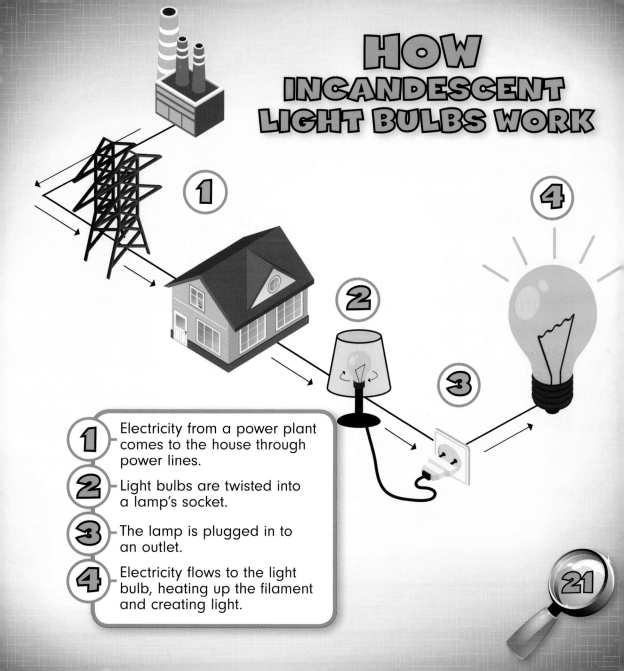

1. Electricity from a power plant comes to the house through power lines.

2. Light bulbs are twisted into a lamp's socket.

3. The lamp is plugged in to an outlet.

4. Electricity flows to the light bulb, heating up the filament and creating light.

GLOSSARY

battery: something placed in a machine to power it with electricity

conduct: to allow electricity to flow through

efficient: able to do something without waste

energy: power used to do work

incandescent: giving off bright light when heated

socket: an opening on something that runs on electricity

vacuum: an empty space from which all air has been taken out

wire: a thin piece of metal often covered with rubber or plastic

FOR MORE INFORMATION

BOOKS

Hord, Colleen. *From Power Plant to House*. Vero Beach, FL: Rourke Educational Media, 2014.

Oxlade, Chris. *The Light Bulb*. Chicago, IL: Heinemann Library/ Capstone, 2012.

Thomas, Elizabeth. *Conserving Energy*. Mankato, MN: The Child's World, 2012.

WEBSITES

How Does a Light Bulb Work?
mocomi.com/how-does-a-light-bulb-work/
Watch a video and read about how the light bulb lights!

How Light Bulbs Work
www.sciencekids.co.nz/videos/engineering/lightbulbs.html
Find out how light bulbs are made here.

INDEX